PETS' GUIDES

Goldie's Guide to

Caring for Your Goldfish

Anita Ganeri

Raintree is an imprint of Capstone Global Library Limited, a company incorporated in England and Wales having its registered office at 7 Pilgrim Street, London, EC4V 6LB – Registered company number: 6695582

To contact Raintree:
Phone: 0845 6044371
Fax: + 44 (0) 1865 312263
Email: myorders@raintreepublishers.co.uk

Outside the UK please telephone +44 1865 312262

Edited by Daniel Nunn, Rebecca Rissman, and Sian Smith
Designed by Cynthia Della-Rovere
Picture research by Tracy Cummins
Original illustrations © Capstone Global Library Ltd 2013
Illustrated by Rick Peterson
Production by Victoria Fitzgerald
Originated by Capstone Global Library Ltd
Printed and bound in China by South China Printing Company Ltd

ISBN 978 1 4062 5059 6 (hardback)
16 15 14 13 12
10 9 8 7 6 5 4 3 2 1

ISBN 978 1 4062 5066 4 (paperback)
17 16 15 14 13
10 9 8 7 6 5 4 3 2 1

British Library Cataloguing in Publication Data
Ganeri, Anita, 1961-
 Goldie's guide to caring for your goldfish. – (Pets' guides)
 1. Goldfish–Juvenile literature.
 I. Title II. Series
 639.3'7484-dc23

Acknowledgements

The author and publisher are grateful to the following for permission to reproduce copyright material: Alamy pp. 21 (© Juniors Bildarchiv), 23 (© Pink Sun Media), 25 (© fishpix); Capstone Library pp. 7, 11, 13, 17, 19, 27 (Karon Dubke); Corbis p. 5 (© Michael Pole); Getty Images p. 9 (Justin Sullivan); iStockphoto p. 15 (© polarica).

Cover photograph of a goldfish reproduced with permission of Superstock (© age fotostock).

We would like to thank Ray Rich, from the Goldfish Society of Great Britain, for his assistance in the preparation of this book.

Every effort has been made to contact copyright holders of material reproduced in this book. Any omissions will be rectified in subsequent printings if notice is given to the publisher.

Disclaimer

Contents

Some words are shown in bold, **like this**. You can find out what they mean by looking in the glossary.

Do you want a pet goldfish?

Hi! I'm Goldie the goldfish, and I'm very pleased to meet you. If you're thinking of getting a goldfish as a pet, you have come to the right place. This book is all about fish like me and what great pets we make!

Goldfish like me need looking after properly for our whole lives. You will need to feed me every day and find me a clean, safe place to live in with plenty of space. Otherwise, I can easily become unhappy and ill.

Choosing your fish

Fish come in lots of different sizes and colours. Common goldfish like me can be golden-red or have patches of yellow, silver, black, or white. Some types of goldfish have long, trailing fins and tails.

You can buy your goldfish from a pet shop, a garden centre, or from a fish **breeder**. Goldfish like living together so you can keep a few of us, as long as your tank is big enough.

Healthy goldfish

Make sure that you pick a healthy goldfish. Watch me swimming about in my tank. If I'm lively and active and my fins are strong and upright, I'm probably a good choice. A fish that has split or damaged fins or is very thin may not be very well.

Your new goldfish should also have shiny skin and bright, clear eyes. Before buying your fish, look around the shop. If the shop is clean and well looked after, it is more likely that the fish will be healthy, too.

Getting ready

Before you bring me home for the first time, you need to get a few things ready. The most important thing to have is a large tank with plenty of room for me to swim about in. Here is the rest of my goldfish home-coming checklist…

Goldie's shopping list

- tap water
- **dechlorinator**
- a **water filter**
- gravel for the bottom of the tank
- **air pump** and **airline**
- water plants
- a small net for moving your goldfish
- a bucket
- goldfish food.

Fitting out a tank

You need to get my tank ready before you bring me home. Two days before I come home, fill my tank with tap water, mixed with **dechlorinator**. Then let the water warm up to **room temperature**. Fix the **water filter** to my tank and keep it turned on all the time. It will keep the water clean and healthy for me.

If my tank has only got water in it, I'll soon get bored with living there. Put some gravel on the bottom to make it more interesting. Stand my tank somewhere away from **draughts** and bright sunlight.

Breathing

Like all animals, I have to breathe a gas called **oxygen** to stay alive. I get oxygen from the water in my tank. To keep the amount of oxygen at just the right level, you need to fix an **air pump** to the tank.

Please also put some water plants in my tank. They make oxygen for me to breathe. I also like to swim about and hide among the leaves. Plant them firmly in the gravel on the bottom of the tank. They look best in groups of tall and short plants.

Welcome home

The day has come for me to move into my new home. The pet shop will give you a large plastic bag filled with water to carry me in. Don't tip me straight into the tank. Otherwise, the shock of the different water temperature could make me ill.

Float the bag in the tank for 20 minutes. Leaving the bag in the water makes sure that the water temperature is the same in the bag as it is in the tank. Then catch me in a net and put me into my new home.

Feeding time

It's time for my breakfast! Feed me special goldfish flakes or **pellets** that you can buy from a pet shop. Sprinkle them on the water. Then watch me swim to the surface to munch up my food.

Please feed me twice a day, in the morning and evening. Take care not to give me too much food. If there is any food left after 15 minutes, scoop it out with a net. Otherwise, it may go bad and make me ill.

Cleaning the tank

Goldfish like me like a nice, clean tank. Bits of old food, dead leaves, and fish poo can make the water dirty. Please check the water every day to make sure that it is clean. I can quickly become ill in a dirty tank.

Every week or two, change half of the water in the tank. Make sure the water you put back is at **room temperature**. Clean the tank thoroughly. Use a scraper to clean any green slime off the inside of the glass.

Fish in ponds

Like all goldfish, I'll grow up and get bigger, so please make sure that my tank is big enough for me and my friends. Goldfish don't like an **overcrowded** tank, so you might have to buy a new, bigger one for us.

wire mesh

If I grow longer than about 12 centimetres, I can't live in a tank anymore. I need to go and live in an outside pond. You might have one in your garden. Cover the pond with wire mesh to stop birds and cats trying to catch me.

Poorly goldfish

If you look after me properly, I should stay healthy for many years. If I start swimming slowly, my fins droop, or I go off my food, I may be ill, so please call the vet. The vet will be able to find out what is wrong with me.

white lump

Look out for white lumps on my body and fins. These are also signs that I may have a nasty illness. The vet will give you some medicine for me, but you may need to move me to my own tank until I'm better.

Going away

If you're going on holiday, please make sure that someone else takes care of me. They should feed me every other day with a small amount of food, and change one-third of the water in my tank about every five days.

Leave your friend a supply of food and everything they need to look after me. Write a note of how much food they should give me. It can make me ill if I eat too much. You should also leave them a telephone number for the vet.

Goldfish facts

- Goldfish were first kept as pets in China more than a thousand years ago. They belong to the carp family.

- The biggest pet goldfish on record measured 48 centimetres long.

- A goldfish usually lives for about 5 to 10 years but the oldest goldfish known is an amazing 49 years old.

- People used to think that goldfish could only remember things for a few seconds. In fact, their memories last for 3 to 5 months.

- Goldfish can learn to recognize different human faces and voices.

Helpful tips

🔵 Feed your goldfish regularly, but do not feed it too much. Your goldfish should always seem to be hungry and should never ignore the food you give it.

🔵 Never keep your goldfish in a goldfish bowl. There would not be enough **oxygen** for your goldfish to breathe and it may die.

🔵 Types of water plants you can put in your tank are:

Elodea – these root in the gravel

Hornwort – these float in the top part of the tank

Duckweed – these float on the surface

🔵 Make sure that your tank is kept covered and out of reach of cats and other pets.

Glossary

airline a tube that carries air from the air pump into your tank

air pump a machine fixed to your tank that puts oxygen in the water for your fish to breathe

breeder someone who keeps goldfish for sale

dechlorinator chemicals you add to the water in your fish tank to make it safe

draughts blasts of cold air that come through windows or under doors

overcrowded when too many things are put into a small space

oxygen a gas that animals need to breathe to stay alive

pellets small lumps of food

room temperature the usual temperature of a room in your home

water filter a machine fixed to your tank that keeps the water clean

Find out more

Books to read

Care for your Goldfish (RSPCA Pet Guide)
  (Collins, 2004)

Goldfish (Pet's Life), Anita Ganeri (Raintree, 2009)

Websites

www.gsgb.co.uk
The Goldfish Society of Great Britain has lots of
information and advice on keeping goldfish.

www.rspca.org.uk
The Royal Society for the Prevention of Cruelty to
Animals gives you information about pets and how
to look after them.

Index

32